Copyright © 2002 Disney Enterprises, Inc.
A Roundtable Press Book
New York

For information, address Disney Editions, 114 Fifth Avenue, New York, New York 10011-5690
Visit www.disneyeditions.com

The following are some of the registered trademarks and service marks owned by Disney Enterprises, Inc.:
Adventureland, California Screamin'®, Critter Country, Disneyland® Hotel, Disneyland® Park, Disneyland® Resort,
Disney's California Adventure™ Park, Disney's Grand Californian Hotel, Disney's Paradise Pier Hotel,
Downtown Disney® District, Fantasyland, Frontierland, Main Street, U.S.A., Mickey's Toontown,
Mission Tortilla Factory®, New Orleans Square, Space Mountain, Splash Mountain, Tomorrowland, Toontown,
Walt Disney World® Resort.

A Bug's Life characters © Disney Enterprises, Inc. and Pixar Animation Studios
Jim Henson's Muppet*Vision 3D ™ & © 2001 The Jim Henson Company
Indiana Jones™ and Star Tours © Lucasfilm Ltd.
Roger Rabbit characters © Disney/Amblin
TARZAN'S TREEHOUSE® is a registered trademark of Edgar Rice Burroughs, Inc. All rights reserved.
Who Wants To Be A Millionaire © Valleycrest Production Ltd.

Text: Tim O'Day and Lorraine Santoli

For Disney Editions
Editorial Director: Wendy Lefkon
Editor and Additional Text: Jody Revenson

For Roundtable Press, Inc.
Directors: Marsha Melnick, Julie Merberg, Susan E. Meyer
Project Coordinator, Computer Production, Photo Editor, Designer: Steven Rosen

ISBN 0-7868-5325-5

First Edition
2 4 6 8 10 9 7 5 3 1

Table of Contents

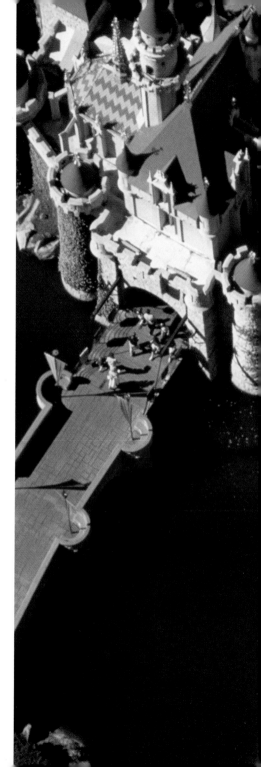

Disney's California Adventure Park™

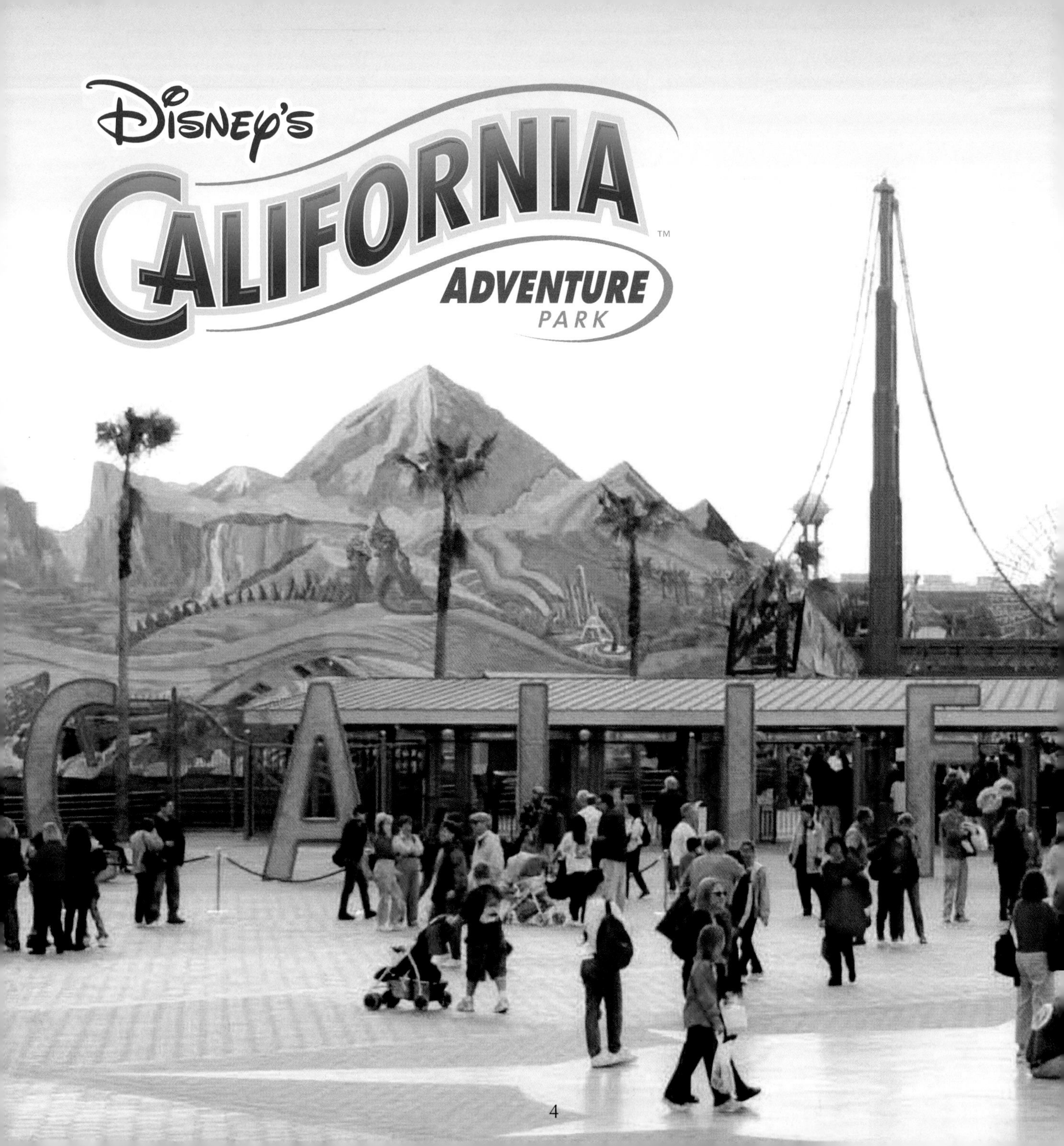

The central theme of the Golden State is diversity—in the land, the history, and the people of California. The area is divided into a variety of regions, all distinctly different in topography, culture, and history. From the northern Sierra to the deserts, the ocean, the valleys, and vineyards, the great breadth of California—its rich heritage and natural beauty—is represented and celebrated throughout Golden State.

Celebrate California's aviation history at Condor Flats. Aircraft memorabilia, weathered airplane hangars, and test equipment are all incorporated into the dusty landscape of this "renewed" high-desert airfield.

DAILY TOUR SCHEDULE
(ALL TIMES APPROXIMATE)

Offering Round-Trip Flites to Heater, Devil's Golf Course, and Zzyyzzxx--

BARSTOW BY SPECIAL ARRANGEMENT ONLY

MONDAY — 10 a.m. to NOON
TUESDAY — 11 a.m. to NOON-THIRTY
WEDNESDAY — ONLY IF I FEEL LIKE IT
THURSDAY — CLOUD BUSTING!
Half-Hour Flites to ALL COMERS, 11 a.m. to NOON
5 bucks or best offer.
Condor Flats Residents Half Price

FRIDAY — GONE FISHIN'!
SATURDAY — GONE FISHIN'!
SUNDAY — GONE FISHIN'!

Fly high above the wonders of California in Soarin' Over California, the most realistic free-flight experience ever created. Guests literally soar over the awesome beauty of Yosemite, glide over a Tahoe ski slope, and race above the desert floor, accompanied by six Air Force Thunderbirds. The feel of the wind over the Golden Gate and the sweet scent of orange blossoms and pine trees over the Redwood forests enhance this incredible journey.

The Grizzly Peak Recreation Area evokes the pristine wilderness and natural beauty of California's state and national parks. Sheltered under the craggy countenance of Grizzly Peak Mountain, a leisurely walk amid towering pine trees and rustic scenery is a delight to the senses, as trails meander over and around landscapes inspired by the High Sierras. The world of California's park rangers is re-created in a fun-filled, high-energy obstacle course set amid a trio of ranger fire towers at the Redwood Creek Challenge Trail.

White-knuckle it down Grizzly River Run on one of the most sophisticated white-water rafting rides of its kind. The wet and wild fun begins as circular rafts float past towering redwoods and around an abandoned mining town before careening over a waterfall into a wild-water rampage that ends with a soaking plunge into an erupting geyser field.

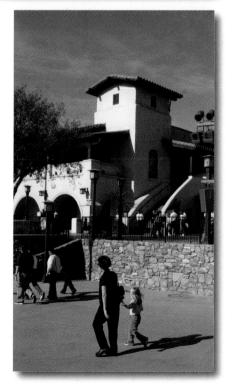

The world-famous Napa Valley provides inspiration for The Golden Vine Winery, nestled against Grizzly Mountain. Guests can stroll through the vineyards or sample new vintages at on-site wine-tasting sessions. The Mission-style buildings are set amid a grapevine-strewn countryside. Dine at the Vineyard Room, where elegant foods and wines are paired with a breathtaking view, or sit under the trees while enjoying "take-out" items from the Wine Country Market.

Bountiful Valley
F A R M

Savor California's rich agricultural heritage in the shade of avocado, almond, and apple trees and a bower of orange, lemon, and grapefruit groves at Bountiful Valley Farm presented by Caterpillar, Inc. Hands-on exhibits educate guests about irrigation techniques, farm machinery, pest control, and the process of getting food from the field to the table. Relax with a frothy cold drink at Sam Andreas Shakes before visiting the Irrigation Station and its playground of spritzing pipes.

CABBAGE

Flik's Fun Fair is a specially designed environment where garden hoses, pebbles, and blades of grass take on huge proportions, and an abandoned umbrella covers a crazy, drive-it-yourself bug car ride. Flik, Hopper, and zillions of wriggling friends star in *It's Tough To Be A Bug!*, a creepy, crawly show that gives guests a "bug's-eye" view of the perils of insect life. The 3-D movie features an abundance of insects, including the most odoriferous member of the bug world, the stinkbug.

The Bay Area district recalls the distinctive architecture of San Francisco. Continual showings of the stirring film *Golden Dreams* are offered in a replica of the Art Deco–style Palace of Fine Arts. Created exclusively for Disney's California Adventure Park, *Golden Dreams* is a powerful, moving film honoring the people whose hopes, dreams, and hard work have shaped California. Queen Califia, the mythical spirit of California, narrates the journey, from the first Native Americans, the arrival of Spanish settlers, the gold rush era, and the building of the railroads, to the immigration of farm workers, and the founding of the movie industry, through the sixties pop culture and the rise of the computer generation.

Inspired by Monterey's Cannery Row, the Pacific Wharf area recognizes the contributions of the many diverse cultures that settled the northern California coastline. On-site workshops and tours demonstrate the assembly-line techniques of the various foods produced in these micro-factories. While walking through the hodgepodge of wood and brick buildings along the industrial waterfront, guests can peek into Boudin Bakery to watch Sourdough Bread being made, see tortillas roll off the line at Mission Tortilla Factory (below), and puzzle over the elaborate fortune cookie-making machinery at The Lucky Fortune Cookery.

The diversity of Pacific Wharf's cuisine offers a wide palate of choices for discriminating gourmands, who can savor their selection on outdoor patios. Enjoy seafood and sandwiches served on oven-fresh Boudin Sourdough French Bread at the Pacific Wharf Café; dim sum, Korean rice dishes, and Chinese egg noodles at The Lucky Fortune Cookery; or specialty tacos wrapped in tortillas from the Mission Tortilla Factory at the Cocina Cucamonga Mexican Grill.

Stargazers get a backstage pass to the glitz and
glamour of moviemaking on the Hollywood
Pictures Backlot, where showbiz-themed
shows, rides, and attractions celebrate
American's ongoing love affair with the movies.
Fun and fantasy prevail as guests get a star's-
eye view of movie madness and experience exciting action
on this re-creation of the ultimate Hollywood movie studio.

Hollywood Pictures Backlot

Step through the enormous ornate Studio gates and find yourself on a palm-lined boulevard of dreams. Classic Los Angeles architecture inspired the buildings that line Disney's Hollywood Boulevard and Backlot areas, which dazzles with stylish Art Deco facades. Even the street glitters underfoot: just like the real Hollywood Boulevard, the asphalt has a shimmering, star-like sparkle. Enjoy a gourmet coffee or frosty smoothie at Schmoozies!, just one of the many tongue-in-cheek dining options on Hollywood Boulevard.

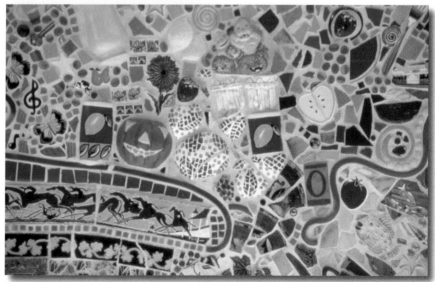

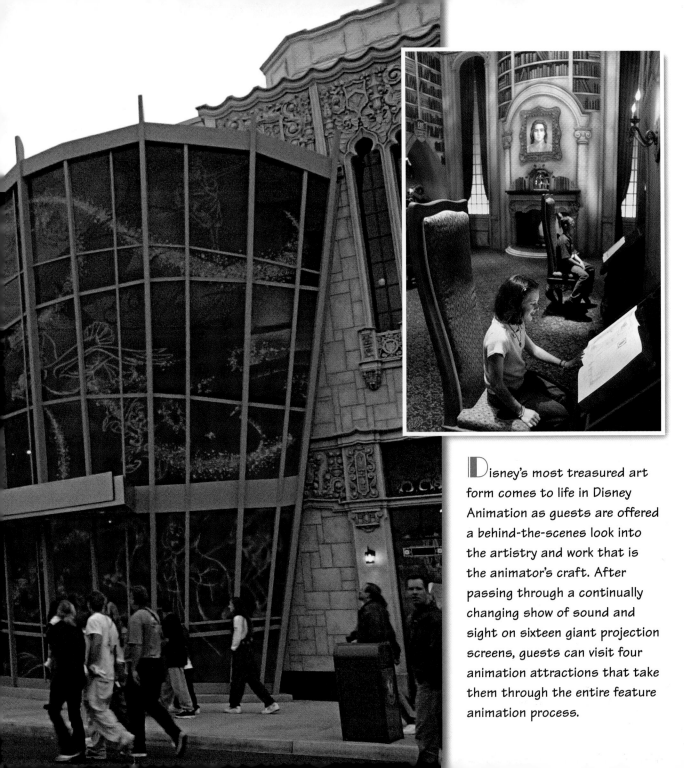

Disney's most treasured art form comes to life in Disney Animation as guests are offered a behind-the-scenes look into the artistry and work that is the animator's craft. After passing through a continually changing show of sound and sight on sixteen giant projection screens, guests can visit four animation attractions that take them through the entire feature animation process.

Set in a lavish showplace reminiscent of the original *Muppet Show* television series, Kermit, Miss Piggy, Fozzie Bear, and a half dozen other Muppets join together in Jim Henson's Muppet*Vision 3D to enlighten spectators on the art and illusion of three-dimensional filmmaking. But things don't always go as planned at their fictional studio's FX Research and Development Lab, and evasive action may be necessary when squirt gun sprays, fireworks, and cream pies appear to fly right out of the screen and into the audience.

RIZZO'S PROP SHOP AND PAWN

njoy delectable dining at the Llanview Country Club and Stables from *One Life to Live*, Adam Chandler's mansion from *All My Children*, The Docks of *Port Charles*, or dish the dirt at Kelly's Diner, Luke's, or the nurse's station from *General Hospital* and view a display of actual wardrobe and props from your favorite shows at the ABC Soap Opera Bistro.

The guest with the fastest finger is chosen from the audience to land in the "hot seat" on the live show attraction Who Wants To Be A Millionaire - Play It! All contestants play for points, not dollars, on a replica of the famous high-tech Who Wants To Be A Millionaire set, complete with its dramatic lighting. Players still have three lifelines for help, but when the guests "phone a friend," the call will go to a complete stranger passing by outside the theater.

Hyperion Theater is the first Broadway-style enclosed theater ever built in a Disney theme park. Recalling the stylish movie houses of Hollywood's golden age, this ornate, 2,000-seat showplace features high-energy, dazzling song-and-dance musical reviews showcasing live entertainment. The exterior facade is patterned after an historic vaudeville theater, but after guests pass through a lobby featuring a wall ornamented with mural panels depicting scenes from life during Hollywood's heyday, the interior is strictly state-of-the-art technology.

Take a madcap, glitzy ride through the star-studded streets of Los Angeles on Superstar Limo, where guests become the most sought-after stars ever to hit the big time. After boarding a purple limousine, you receive a frantic call on the video cell phone telling you to rush to a big movie premiere! Along the way you'll zoom past the famous landmarks of Rodeo Drive and Sunset Strip, encounter a Malibu mud slide, and cruise through the affluent neighborhoods of Beverly Hills and Bel Air as you careen toward a happy ending as Hollywood's newest star.

The super high-energy zone of Disney's California Adventure Park, Paradise Pier is a glittering amusement district inspired by some of the Golden State's most famous beachfront parks such as the Long Beach Pike, Santa Cruz Boardwalk, and Pacific Ocean Park. A monument to sun, surf, and sand, the area epitomizes California beach culture. The sights and sounds are nostalgic, but the excitement and technology are very much present-day. It's an atmosphere pulsing with action at every turn.

Paradise Pier

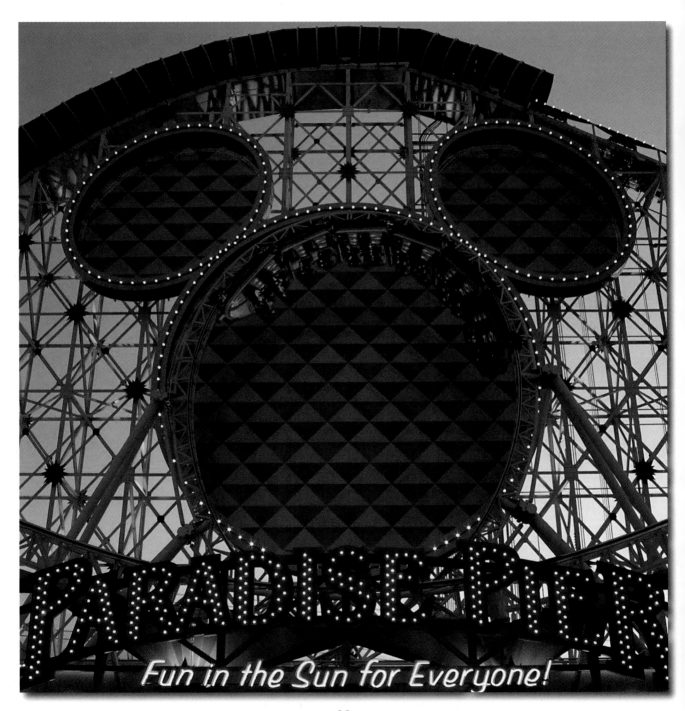

38

The California Screamin' roller coaster provides high-intensity thrills and white-knuckle chills when it literally catapults guests from zero to fifty-five mph in a five-second incline before sending its passengers over, under, and around a 6,000-foot, steel-reinforced track. Every twist and turn is synchronized to a pounding sound track as riders race over the midway games area and boardwalk. The ride climaxes with a 360-degree loop around a giant stylized Mickey Mouse head.

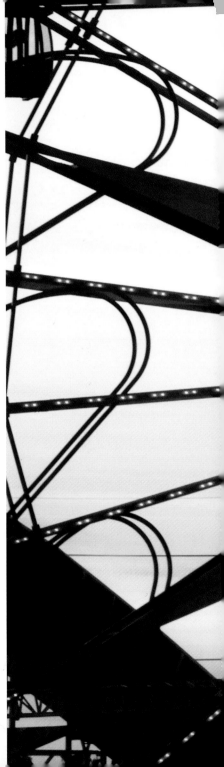

The celestial-faced Sun Wheel features a ride-in-a-ride like no other within its 150-foot diameter. Passengers can view the entire park from across the four-acre bay as they ride in this beautifully designed Wonder Wheel, one of only three spinning wheels that exist in the world. Sixteen of the wheel's 24 six-person gondolas actually slide in, out, and around on tracks laced within the diameter of the outer wheel. Its friendly, beaming sun face and blinking lights make it one of the park's most recognizable icons.

The Orange Stinger giant swing ride has lots of "a-peel" as guests ride in faster and faster circles inside the sphere of a half-peeled California orange. As passengers buzz along, picking up speed, a lone droning bee on the sound track is joined by others until the entire citrus-scented interior reverberates with the sound of a swarming hive.

Swing the mallet, ring the bell, win a prize! The Maliboomer takes the strength-testing games of years past a giant step further as it catapults guests skyward 180 feet in only two seconds in its jet-lift carriages. Then, bungee-like, passengers slowly bounce back to earth—and catch their breath—on one of the ride's three towers. At night, glowing yellow, blue, pink, and purple lights add to the dizzying fun.

Young thrill seekers sit in brightly colored jellyfish-shaped vehicles in the Jumpin' Jellyfish, a kiddie version of a vertical parachute ride. After rising to the top of a 50-foot tower, the bell of the jellyfish unfolds and its tentacles fly in the wind as passengers float slowly back to the ground-level kelp bed.

Carousels are the heart of any boardwalk, and King Triton's Carousel is quintessentially Californian. Riders are carried on hand-painted ocean creatures including sea lions, otters, whales, and dolphins, while a classic band organ plays 1960s-style surf songs.

Described as "the world's smallest, slowest, most terrifying roller coaster," Mulholland Madness sends guests through a California map book cover onto a wacky trip over the California freeway system from the Hollywood Hills to Malibu. Each four-seater car parodies a classic West Coast vehicle as it winds through a landscape of sight gags and freeway frolics.

Climb aboard the Golden Zephyr for a nostalgic and exhilarating swing-ride. Passengers are spun in a wide arc over Paradise Pier Bay as they sit in one of six steel-and-chrome futuristic spaceships that are suspended by cables from a rotating 85-foot tower. A gleaming, sun-lit spectacular attraction by day, the Golden Zephyr is illuminated by sparkling rim lights and the Paradise Pier logo at night.

Avalon Cove, with its whimsical sand castle design, hosts seaside supping with some of Disney's best-loved characters. Classic seaside amusement is brought into the present day as the Boardwalk leads guests onto the Midway and its exciting games of skill and chance (right). The aroma of cotton candy fills the air, and a sideshow sense of play prevails as the California Screamin' roller coaster rattles above the fun.

Disney's Eureka! A California Parade (right) celebrates the cultural diversity of California in a colorful and entertaining extravaganza. A pageant of nearly 100 performers, puppets, and towering parade units weaves its way around the park, making performance stops where guests can interact with the theatrical experience. With more than half-a-million lightbulbs sparkling in a procession over a quarter mile long, Disney's Electrical Parade (left and below) offers dazzling fun. Its brilliant tiny lights transform the performers and floats into fanciful scenes from Walt Disney film classics to the sounds of its distinctive sound track, "Baroque Hoedown."

Family-friendly resorts, world-class shopping, and high-energy entertainment complement the fun at the hotels and marketplaces of the Disneyland Resort. Disney's Grand Californian Hotel provides a spectacular view of the excitement at Disney's California Adventure Park and, along with the Disneyland Hotel and Disney's Paradise Pier Hotel, presents endless opportunities for great dining, invigorating recreation, and souvenir shopping. Downtown Disney offers an enticing public esplanade of themed dining, sophisticated shopping, and family-oriented entertainment.

Disneyland® Resort Hotels and Downtown Disney®

Disney's Grand Californian Hotel, the first-ever hotel-within-a-Disney theme park, captures the romantic style of the California Arts and Crafts era in its distinctive architecture, luxurious rooms, and charming recreational amenities. In addition to a cozy, hearth-side lounge and sequoia-lined courtyard, saunas and massages are offered at a state-of-the-art health club. The Napa Rose (right) serves the finest dishes from the state's bountiful seacoasts and farms in an elegant setting that celebrates the wine country.

Comfortable and casual, Disney's Paradise Pier Hotel offers relaxation, family dining, and spectacular views of Disney's California Adventure Park. Guests can have breakfast with Minnie and friends (above left), as well as soak in a soothing spa, take a dip in the rooftop pool, or work out at Team Mickey's. The hotel's two high-rise towers are juxtaposed to create a central atrium, which cradles the lobby and a larger-than-life character sculpture.

Goofy greets guests arriving at the Disneyland Hotel, located on Magic Way. The hotel features fun restaurants and premier shopping, plus three swimming pools and a sandy beach. The magical Never Land pool, based on the animated classic *Peter Pan*, showcases Captain Hook's pirate ship and Skull Rock, where adventurous guests can ride down a 110-foot-long water slide. At night, the resort comes alive with exciting entertainment, including live music at the host bar and Fantasy Waters, a display of water fountains and colorful lights choreographed to a medley of Disney tunes.

Downtown Disney District provides dining, shopping, and high-energy entertainment, set in a luxuriant landscape filled with nearly 200 species of plants amid its eclectic architecture. Linking the old park with the new, the Disney Imagineers who created Downtown Disney combined Old World ambience with contemporary American energy. At the center of Paradise Plaza, a fountain shaped like a California poppy (the state flower) adds coolness to the hot live-music area. Many Downtown Disney venues serve double (and triple) duty as dining and dancing—and sometimes shopping—spots.

Step onto Main Street, U.S.A., and suddenly the stress of contemporary life gives way to the quaint and reassuring charms of turn-of-the-century America. Time seems to slow and soften amid the smells of freshly baked muffins and candies, the steady clip-clop of the horse-drawn streetcar, and the twinkling pin-lights outlining the gingerbread trim of the buildings. It is the essence of the hometown America that greeted the dawn of the 20th Century.

Main Street, U.S.A.®

The hub of all Main Street transportation can be found in Town Square. From here guests can travel in style up Main Street in an open-air Horse-Drawn Streetcar, Main Street Fire Engine, Horseless Carriage, or double-decker Omnibus. At the Main Street Station, the four authentic steam trains of the Disneyland Railroad take guests on a grand circle tour of the Magic Kingdom. During the excursion, guests travel along the rim of the Grand Canyon and journey through the incredible Primeval World.

Main Street bustles with a variety of turn-of-the-century experiences for adventurous guests. Town Square is the civic center of this enchanting Victorian "hometown," which features daily concerts by the Disneyland Band and rides on Disneyland Fire Department No. 105 firetruck. The Walt Disney Story Featuring Great Moments with Mr. Lincoln now features a more lived-in Honest Abe who refers to handheld notes as guests listen to his speech delivered through surround sound-enhanced head phones.

The popular animated windows of the Emporium and the mouth-watering sights behind the windows of the Candy Palace and Candy Kitchen help make Main Street, U.S.A. a window-shopper's paradise. Along Main Street you can easily find the perfect gift or souvenir—from traditional Mickey Mouse "ears" and Disney collectibles of the past to fanciful silhouettes made while you wait.

I n Adventureland your senses are stirred by the sights of lush jungle foliage, the sounds of wild animals, and the aromas of tropical blossoms. This realm of adventure and exploration is an amazing amalgam of many of the world's far-off places and uncharted regions. One quick turn can lead to the exotic rivers of the world (Jungle Cruise), the hot sands of the Middle East (Aladdin's Oasis), the vastness of Africa (Tarzan's Treehouse), the tropical magic of Polynesia (Walt Disney's Enchanted Tiki Room), or the steamy jungles of India (Indiana Jones™ Adventure).

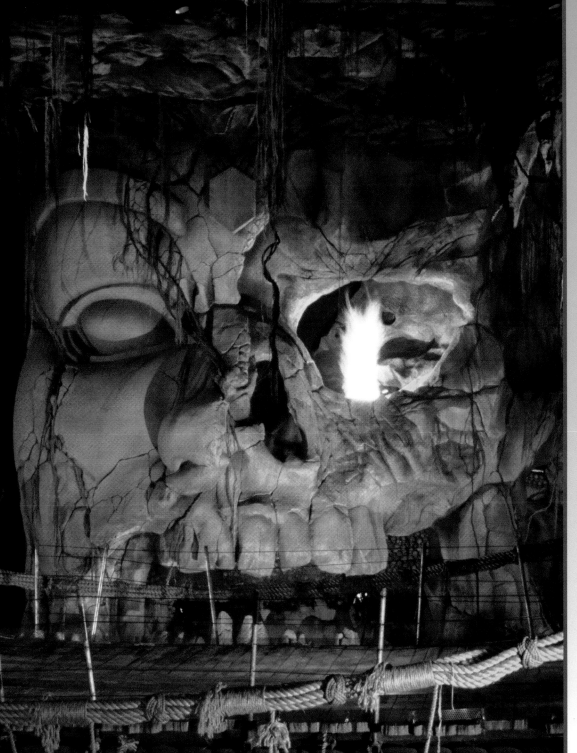

Adventureland®

Join Professor Jones deep in the heart of India for the Indiana Jones™ Adventure. It's 1935 and discovery awaits in the Temple of the Forbidden Eye. Brave guests board well-worn troop transports that take them into a strange, subterranean world where they have an unfortunate encounter with the mysterious temple deity Mara in the great Chamber of Destiny. Forced to flee, guests narrowly escape a collapsing bridge, giant snakes, thousands of rats, booby-traps, and the prospect of being crushed by a 5-ton boulder!

Cross over a rickety suspension bridge to Tarzan's Treehouse, which celebrates the high-flying escapades of the "Lord of the Apes." Based on the hit Disney animated film *Tarzan*™, this climb-through adventure 70-feet above Adventureland allows guests to scale Tarzan's treetop home and relive many of the film's exciting and memorable moments. At the base of the tree, kids can "trash the camp" in an interactive area filled with shipwreck supplies. Occasionally, live animals and well-known characters such as Tarzan, Jane, and even the rambunctious gorilla Terk greet guests as they exit the treehouse.

The Jungle Cruise has hosted millions of would-be explorers aboard its thrilling excursions into the jungle. From the safety of your launch, witness the gathering of animals on the African Veldt or perhaps catch a rare glimpse of the "Lost Safari," a group of unfortunate adventurers who always seem to be in the company of an angry rhino.

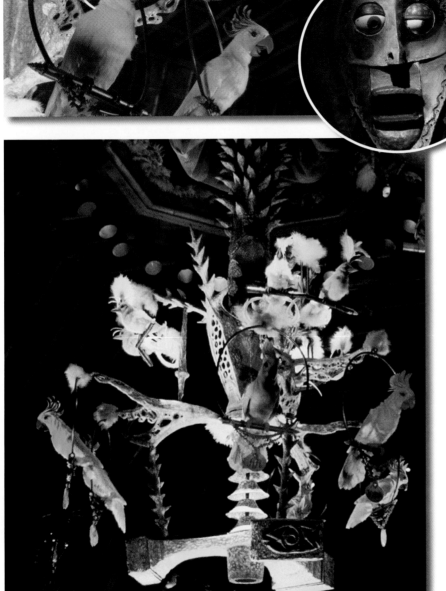

Walt Disney's Enchanted Tiki Room entertains Adventureland guests with its irreverent presentation in which "the birdies sing and the flowers croon." The macaw hosts of the show—José, Michael, Fritz, and Pierre—have welcomed hundreds of thousands of guests into their special "world of joyous songs and wondrous miracles."

More than 225 birds, flowers, and tikis delight the audience with the melodious Enchanted Fountain, some Offenbach tunes, and a rousing rendition of "Let's All Sing Like the Birdies Sing." According to the birds, their show is designed to "fill you with pleasure and glee because if we don't make you feel like that, we're gonna wind up on a lady's hat!"

The breathtaking sight of the gleaming white *Mark Twain* riverboat or the imposing gallantry of the *Columbia* sailing ship as it approaches the dock beckons guests into Frontierland, a robust panorama of America's pioneer past. As soon as you pass through the stockade entrance, you are surrounded by an amalgam of sights and sounds that authentically conjures up images from America's western expansion, from the bustling riverfronts of the Mississippi and Missouri rivers to the dusty southwestern desert of the mid-1800s.

FRONTIERLAND®

The Rivers of America in Frontierland provides a variety of ways for would-be pioneers of all ages to explore the wilderness outposts of the backwoods. The dazzling white *Mark Twain* riverboat carries guests upriver in southern elegance, while the 84-foot-tall, 10-gun, 3-masted *Columbia* sailing ship lets passengers relive life aboard an authentic replica of the first American ship to sail around the world. Guests get a close-up look at river life as they ride the backwaters of the Rivers of America.

Big Thunder Mountain Railroad—
"the wildest ride in the wilderness!"
—whisks brave guests back to
the gold rush era. Hop aboard
runaway mine trains and race
around towering buttes, dive into
dangerous gulches, and plunge deep
into foreboding caverns filled with
bats and phosphorescent pools.
The reckless trains careen past
raging waterfalls, splash through
still waters, and finally encounter a
deafening earthquake from which
the mountain gets its name.

Log rafts transport guests across the Rivers of America to Tom Sawyer Island, an oasis of adventure where kids of all ages can follow in the footsteps of Tom, Huck Finn, and Becky Thatcher. Guests can explore the foreboding Injun Joe's Cave, visit Smuggler's Cove, splash across Barrel Bridge, or keep a lookout for river pirates from the sentry posts of Fort Wilderness®.

On select nights, the Rivers of America in Frontierland erupts into the night-time spectacular FANTASMIC! One of the most complex and technically advanced shows ever presented at Disneyland Park, this hugely popular extravaganza features a battle of good and evil inside Mickey Mouse's fanciful imagination, highlighting scenes from Disney's animated classics, including *Fantasia, Peter Pan, Beauty and the Beast,* and *Sleeping Beauty.*

Here is the Paris of the American frontier, the Crescent City of New Orleans as it was 150 years ago. Within its sheltered courtyards and winding streets, elegance and charm mingle comfortably with the almost constant and irreverent sounds of Dixieland jazz. Beneath its ornate wrought-iron balconies are some of the most distinctive restaurants and shops in Disneyland Park. This bend of the river also plays host to two signature Disneyland attractions—Pirates of the Caribbean and the Haunted Mansion.

New Orleans Square®

"Set sail with the wildest crew that ever sacked the Spanish Main" aboard the memorable high-seas adventure, Pirates of the Caribbean. You'll encounter fun-loving rogues in search of treasure, but be warned that "Dead Men Tell No Tales." From the rambunctious buccaneers plundering a seaport village to the mysterious grottoes of Davy Jones's Locker, Pirates of the Caribbean is an adventure for seafarers of all ages.

"Welcome, foolish mortals, to the Haunted Mansion," home to 999 frightfully funny ghosts and happy haunts—but there is always room for one more! There is no shortage of hot- and cold-running chills in this stately antebellum mansion —each room is furnished with wall-to-wall creaks. All the spirits are "just dying to meet you," as you tour the house in your own private "Doom Buggy." But beware of hitchhiking ghosts—they just may try to follow you home!

estled in a lazy corner of the backwoods is Critter Country. Here, amid shady trees and cool streams, is a world where the rabbits, bears, opossums, foxes, alligators, owls, and frogs are just as social and neighborly as they can be. Keen eyes might spot wily Brer Rabbit outsmarting Brer Fox and Brer Bear atop Chickapin Hill while guests drift through the swamps and bayous inside Splash Mountain, before spilling into a briar-laced pond five stories below the peak.

Critter Country®

Every day is a "Zip-a-Dee-Doo-Dah" kind of day in Critter Country. Here you can savor long lazy afternoons in the shade or simply delight in the rustic country atmosphere. Enjoy down-home dining at the Hungry Bear Restaurant along the river's edge or quench your thirst in the Brer Bar. At the Briar Patch, you can find items suitable for decorating any den, cave, or home.

Hop aboard one of Davy Crockett's Explorer Canoes for an exciting paddle-powered excursion around the Rivers of America. Crashing through the wake of the mighty *Mark Twain* and having a thrilling encounter with an authentic encampment of Plains Indians along the riverbank are only part of the adventure in this hands-on exploration of the frontier.

Inspired by Walt Disney's classic film *Song of the South* and the wise fables of Uncle Remus, Splash Mountain provides brave guests with a chance to follow in the perilous footsteps of wily Brer Rabbit. Search for your "Laughing Place" as you journey through this exciting flume adventure featuring five drops, including a hair-raising finale that sends you on a 52-foot, 45-degree angle, 40-mph plunge into a watery briar patch.

Cross over the moat and through the archways of Sleeping Beauty Castle to enter "the happiest kingdom of them all"—Fantasyland. Enchanted tales of childhood adapted from Walt Disney's classic animated films come to life in this timeless realm of the imagination. Within the magical Old World setting, guests can fly through the London night to Never Land, see an elephant fly, take a spin in a giant teacup, and brave the icy thrills of the Matterhorn.

Fantasyland®

$\mathcal{O}$ne of the most photographed and familiar icons in the park, Sleeping Beauty Castle has stood guard over Fantasyland since the opening of Disneyland Park in 1955. The Bavarian-style castle stands like a regal sentinel in shades of pink and blue, a nod to the princess for whom the castle is named. Sharp-eyed guests will notice such details as Walt Disney's family crest above the castle entrance and real 22-karat gold plating adorning the spires. Walt Disney recalled that European castles of old were often built to intimidate the peasants. He believed a less imposing castle would appear friendlier and more inviting to Disneyland guests, and thus Sleeping Beauty Castle is smaller than any of the other Disney theme park castles.

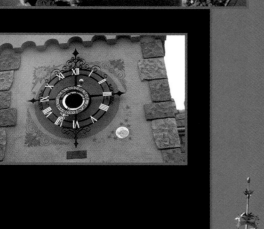

*E*nter Peter Pan's Flight and step aboard your own flying pirate galleon to sail through the Darling nursery and out over London. Follow Tinker Bell toward the "second star to the right" and straight on to Never Land. Passing amid twinkling stars, you'll look down to spy such Never Land locales as Mermaid Lagoon and Skull Rock. After a harrowing encounter with the villainous Captain Hook, you'll join Peter Pan, Wendy, Michael, John, and Tinker Bell as their pixie-dusted galleon sails into the evening sky.

𝒫inocchio's Daring Journey is sure to captivate your heart with its well-loved story of the lonely wood-carver Geppetto and his desire to have a real son. Along cobblestone alpine roads, guests follow little Pinocchio and his faithful conscience Jiminy Cricket as they attempt to avoid fateful encounters with the wily Foulfellow and Gideon the Coachman, and Monstro the Whale. Guided by the "wishing star," guests meet the lovely Blue Fairy and ultimately share in Pinocchio's happy ending.

S ite of numerous wedding proposals, the Snow White Wishing Well and Grotto provides a tranquil and romantic setting along the east side of the Sleeping Beauty Castle moat. The marble figures of Snow White and the Seven Dwarfs were a gift to Walt Disney from an Italian sculptor. Sharp-eared guests can hear Snow White's plaintive refrain of "I'm Wishing" echoing in the depths of the well.

J oin madcap adventurer J. Thaddeus Toad inside stately Toad Hall as he test drives his all-new motorcar and takes everyone on a "wild ride" across the English countryside and to "Nowhere in Particular." This is one of the most beloved

Fantasyland attractions, where guests can race, leap, and crash their way through Mr. Toad's trials and tribulations.

Guests who venture on Snow White's Scary Adventures enter a timeless tale of romance. Here the lovable Seven Dwarfs celebrate with a "Silly Song," and the evil Queen transforms herself into a villainous witch and offers Snow White a juicy apple laced with "the sleeping death." With the arrival of the Prince and love's first kiss, everyone lives happily ever after.

Don't be late for a very important date! Board your very own private Caterpillar and journey down the rabbit hole to join little Alice on her marvelous adventures. Unique to Disneyland Park, the Alice in Wonderland adventure is filled with memorable characters and scenes such as the Unbirthday Party, Tweedledum and Tweedledee, the Garden of Flowers, and the March of the Cards. You can even join in a fateful round of croquet with the ever-explosive Queen of Hearts.

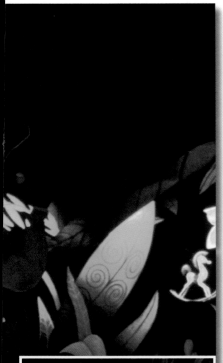

$\mathcal{A}$board the Mad Tea Party, guests can spin and spin and spin their cup and saucer in any direction in this life-size Unbirthday Party. With colorful Chinese paper lanterns hanging overhead and the familiar strains of the "Unbirthday Song" in the air, guests will surely feel as if they had stepped right into the memorable Disney film or the beloved storybook.

Guests aboard the Casey Jr. Circus Train will cheer along as Casey proclaims, "I think I can, I think I can, I think I can," while he chugs and puffs his way through the hills and valleys of Storybook Land. Aboard the Storybook Land Canal Boats, guests glide past miniature homes and settings of Disney's most adored characters.

*G*uests have been captivated by "it's a small world" since it first premiered at the park in 1966. A salute to the children of the world, this delightful attraction speaks the international language of goodwill. Its impressive exterior playfully represents landmarks from around the world, including France's Eiffel Tower, Italy's Leaning Tower of Pisa, and India's famed Taj Mahal. Aboard their boats, guests journey beyond the Topiary Garden and drift with the tide into "the Happiest Cruise That Ever Sailed."

Soar high over Fantasyland aboard Dumbo the Flying Elephant, the world's most famous flying pachyderm. Timothy Mouse watches over this mechanical marvel, full of filigreed metalwork and cogs, gears, and pulleys galore. A European manufacturer of circus organs built the attraction's vintage mechanical band; the organ, constructed circa 1915, weighs three-quarters of a ton and resounds with circuslike music.

The glittering King Arthur Carrousel beckons guests through the archway of Sleeping Beauty Castle. The classic carrousel horses are 90 to 110 years old and are hand-carved and hand-painted; no two are exactly alike. The turntable for the carrousel was made around 1875 and came from Canada. Most of the 19th-century horses were hand-carved in Germany.

Towering 14 stories above Fantasyland, the snow-capped Matterhorn (a 1/100 scale replica of its Swiss namesake) is the breathtaking setting for a thrilling race through ominous ice caves and a frightening chance encounter with the Abominable Snowman. Waterfalls thunder down its icy slopes, which also feature Alpine forests and tranquil ponds. The Matterhorn Bobsleds have their origin in the 1959 Disney film *The Third Man on the Mountain*.

Bursting with color and frenetic energy, Mickey's Toontown is a 1930s classic Disney cartoon come to wacky life. Here in this "toon" social hub, animated stars such as Mickey Mouse, Minnie Mouse, Donald Duck, Goofy, Chip 'n' Dale, and Roger Rabbit live, work, and play, much to the delight of guests of all ages. From the bustle of its downtown to the charm of its residential neighborhood, Mickey's Toontown is a slice of "reel" life where virtually everything has a unique character and personality.

JOLLY TROLLEY

Mickey's Toontown®

The welcome mat is always out at Mickey's House and Meet Mickey. Inside the California bungalow home guests can see where Mickey unwinds and view mementos of his famed career. Mickey himself is at work on a new film project in Mickey's Movie Barn out back. Guests are welcome to drop in to say hello and browse through the collection of props from some of his most famous film roles.

Minnie's House is painted in romantic hues of lavender and pink, and is cozily situated right next door to Mickey's. Inside Minnie's House, guests can play with her computerized vanity, bang out a tune on her pots and pans in the kitchen, or assist her with baking a cake for Mickey. Outside, guests can see her colorful garden and make a wish in her charming wishing well.

The home of Chip 'n' Dale, Donald Duck's mischievous chipmunk adversaries, is appropriately nestled in a colorful acorn tree. Here little guests can meet Chip 'n' Dale and explore their treetop home (above). Nearby in the middle of Toon Lake is Donald's Boat—the *Miss Daisy* (right). Home to the irascible Donald Duck, the boat gives little sailors the opportunity to clang bells and blow whistles.

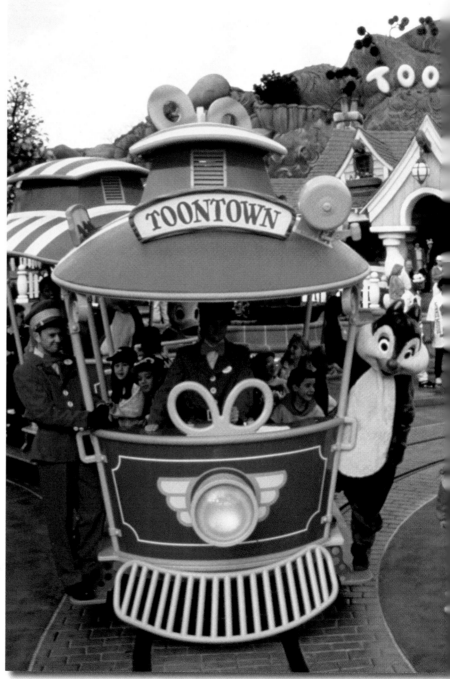

The bright red-and-gold-trimmed Jolly Trolley provides a rambling two-way trip through all of Mickey's Toontown, winding around Roger Rabbit's fountain in Downtown Toontown, traveling into Mickey's Neighborhood, and circling Mickey's fountain. A large gold windup key on top of the engine turns as the trolley runs, and a Tooned-up chassis gives the trolley an ambling, cartoon-like gait.

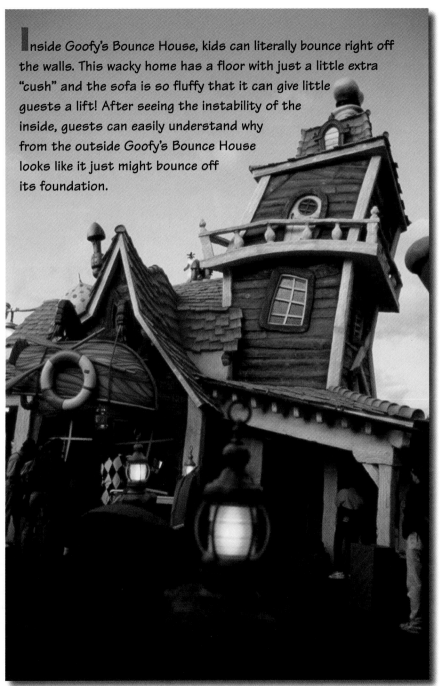

Inside Goofy's Bounce House, kids can literally bounce right off the walls. This wacky home has a floor with just a little extra "cush" and the sofa is so fluffy that it can give little guests a lift! After seeing the instability of the inside, guests can easily understand why from the outside Goofy's Bounce House looks like it just might bounce off its foundation.

Gadget's Go-Coaster, located next to Donald's Boat on Toon Lake, is a high-speed, splash-down contraption for children of all ages. Made from what appear to be large spools, springs, rubber bands, and other assorted household goods, this little coaster is sure to give guests to Mickey's Toontown a beautiful view along with a few butterflies in their stomachs.

Aboard Roger Rabbit's Car Toon Spin, guests ride along with Lenny the Cab as Roger tries to save his lovely Jessica from the dastardly Weasels and a fateful plunge in the deadly "Dip." On this twirling and whirling adventure, guests take a wacky trip through cartoon back alleys in their quest to avoid the Dip and save Jessica and all the citizens of Toontown.

Cross over into Tomorrowland and embark on an exciting journey into "Imagination and Beyond." This intriguing realm of discovery and wonder was inspired by such classic futurists as Jules Verne, H. G. Wells, and Leonardo da Vinci, along with modern visionaries such as George Lucas and Walt Disney. With its whirling spaceships, zooming rocket vehicles, lush vegetation, and kinetic sculptures and fountains, Tomorrowland is an exciting look beyond the stars to a future full of promise and hope.

Tomorrowland®

Pilot your own spaceship aboard the Astro Orbitor and soar through a fantastic, animated "astronomical model" of planets and constellations. With its colorful rockets circling a series of moving planets, the Astro Orbitor is a radiant and impressive kaleidoscope of colors in tones of burnished copper and brass.

You may have a change of perspective in the hilarious 3-D film experience *Honey, I Shrunk the Audience*. All seems well when Professor Wayne Szalinski is presented with the "Inventor of the Year" award from the Imagination Institute. But things go a bit awry when one of his inventions ultimately "shrinks" the audience.

Autopia now enjoys an energizing overhaul with new car designs, new roadways, and an experience of viewing the world as seen by the cars themselves. Go around curves, over bridges, through a "Car Park," and off road in a series of exciting adventures, once the checkered flag is waved.

Tomorrowland's landmark Carousel Theater, which previously housed the former Carousel of Progress and America Sings attractions, is now home to Innoventions, which features products and concepts from the world's leading industries The interactive section of the attraction includes presentations and hands-on displays showcasing creative uses of tomorrow's technology. Guests then flow to a center atrium where they ascend to the upper-level concept presentations, all clustered around an impressive illuminating tree that is literally "wired" for the future.

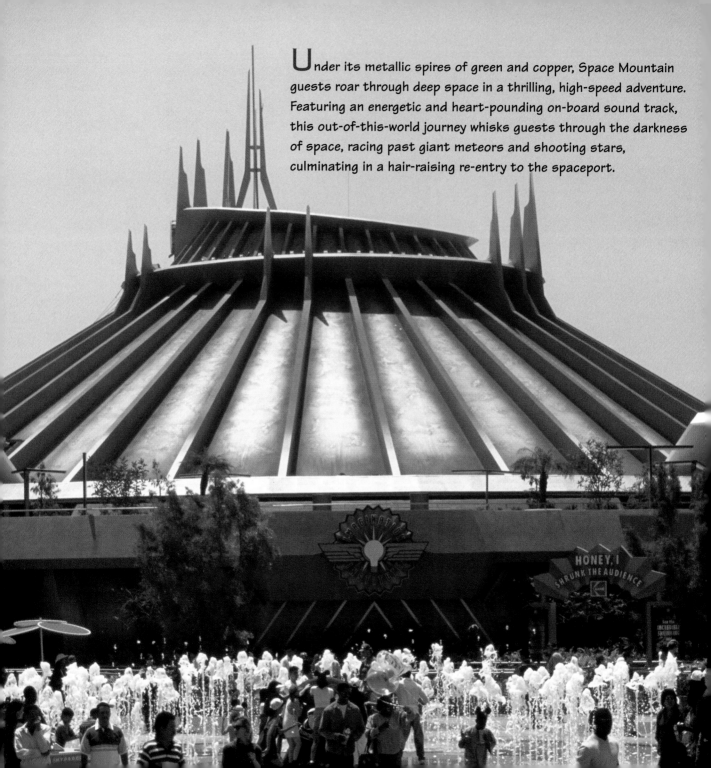

Under its metallic spires of green and copper, Space Mountain guests roar through deep space in a thrilling, high-speed adventure. Featuring an energetic and heart-pounding on-board sound track, this out-of-this-world journey whisks guests through the darkness of space, racing past giant meteors and shooting stars, culminating in a hair-raising re-entry to the spaceport.

HONEY, I
SHRUNK THE AUDIENCE

Inside Star Tours, guests experience a bustling, intergalactic travel agency and spaceport where they soon find themselves aboard a StarSpeeder 3000 on a perilous journey to the moon of Endor. Based on George Lucas's famed film series, Star Tours is a harrowing trip through the cosmos, guided by Rex (a rookie pilot), R2-D2, and C-3PO. Along the way, passengers survive a wild trip through an asteroid, narrowly escape an intergalactic dogfight, and successfully maneuver through the dangerous chasms of a Death Star.